RHYTHM
& BEAUTY

RHYTHM & BEAUTY

THE ART OF PERCUSSION

ROCKY MAFFIT

FOREWORD BY EVELYN GLENNIE / PHOTOGRAPHY BY CHRIS BROWN

WATSON-GUPTILL PUBLICATIONS · NEW YORK

Senior Editor: Bob Nirkind
Designer: Evelyn C. Shapiro
Production Manager: Ellen Greene
Project Editors: Becky Mead and Julie Mazur

This book has been typeset in Hiroshige for text,
with Lithos and Gill Sans Condensed for display type.
The photographs were taken using Mamiya and Rodenstock lenses,
with Fuji Provia films in both 120 and 4 x 5 formats.

First published in 1999 by Watson-Guptill Publications,
a division of BPI Communications, Inc.,
1515 Broadway, New York, NY 10036

Library of Congress Catalog Card Number: 98-89219

ISBN 0-8230-8406-X

Printed in China

First printing, 1999

1 2 3 4 5 6 7 8 9 / 07 06 05 04 03 02 01 00 99

For

Kate,

Jacob, and Walker

CONTENTS

FOREWORD

People often ask me why I decided to take up percussion. It's difficult to say why exactly. I encountered no exceptional musical sounds during my upbringing in northeast Scotland and I can only think that curiosity drew my attention to what I soon discovered is an enormous family of instruments. My enthusiasm may have dated back to when I went to a local talent show and saw a young girl playing the xylophone. She was brilliant, just amazing, and I thought, "I didn't realize a xylophone could do this." Once I went to school, I found there were many more percussion instruments to discover. Percussion doesn't just consist of a xylophone, as I first thought; add over 599 other objects that can be struck, shaken, rattled, and squeezed, and you have a clearer idea of its range.

Now is an especially exciting time. We have been experiencing an explosion in world percussion with all the current awareness of world music. It has been a huge shock to me, discovering the great variety of percussion instruments out there—all those voices and traditions. New techniques and repertoire are continually being developed and percussionists are constantly coming out with innovative, interesting approaches.

Rhythm and Beauty: The Art of Percussion is an ideal introduction to this amazing collection of instruments. I would have loved a book like this when I was starting out—something to deepen my experience and open my eyes. Rocky Maffit's feeling is like my own, a profound joy and exuberance in music and making music. We're both trying to open up a window to the world of percussion and all its many variations, its soul. And we both want people to see, and feel, the possibility to be discovered in this ever-expanding family of instruments. Its infinite variety is far from exhausted, and is only beginning to be appreciated.

Playing percussion, to a great part, takes imagination. If I come across an instrument that I've never heard before, I'll treat it as a child would—I'll play with sticks or my hands and create my own sound palette. I try to find the heartbeat, the vibrations, the inner energy of the instrument—something I can work with in my performances. As I tour, playing in concerts all over the world, my goal is always to express the amazing vitality and range of percussion as well as my passion for music. You will find that in this book as well.

A wonderful thing about percussion is that if you travel around the world you can be assured of discovering traditional and nontraditional instruments everywhere. And while spoken language may be a barrier, there is always a drum that links us together.

—Evelyn Glennie
Cambridgeshire, United Kingdom

A JOURNEY BEGINS

I love percussion. Not only for the sounds, which are myriad and wonderful, but also for the visual and tactile pleasure these instruments give. I am especially drawn to instruments that are closely rooted to natural sounds and the natural world. Percussion can be a unique expression of culture, or reflect the crossing of musical and geographical boundaries. Tambourines, for example, are found in countless countries throughout the world. Conga drums are played in Nashville as well as Nairobi. Most societies have percussion music, just as most have vocal music. There is something essential in our musical natures that motivates us to sing—and to drum.

I spend some part of every year giving lecture-demonstrations on percussion. The seeds of this book were planted by students and teachers who wanted to know more about the instruments in my programs. In my search to refer them to other materials, I discovered many wonderful books on the subject of percussion, but none where picture, text, and sound were combined as I envisioned.

This book and its accompanying recording are an introduction to the sounds, the sources, and the physical beauty of the world of percussion. It is a personal and highly subjective view—probably as notable for what it omits as for what it includes.

Rather than being a musical encyclopedia, this book is the beginning of a journey that may lead you to other resources—not only to books, but also to other percussionists and their recordings, and to instrument makers and purveyors who specialize in percussion.

Here you will encounter the percussion of many countries and cultures. Some instruments are antiques, others are contemporary. Some are handmade while others are produced in factories. Some represent venerated traditions, while others are attempts to expand upon and evolve from tradition. They all, however, are part of a found and forged world of sound, noise, rhythm, and beauty that is the expression of human life.

—Rocky Maffit
Champaign, Illinois

TONAL

PERCUSSION

I f rhythm is the heart of life, then melody is its soul.

When one thinks of percussion, drums naturally come to mind. But percussion is a vast musical universe of which drums are but a part. Its scope ranges from the grandest concert piano to the most humble of seedpod shakers; within this realm, rhythm and melody are inextricably linked.

One of the highest compliments to musicians is to say they make their instruments "sing." Of course, human beings are not the only melodists. Insects, mammals, cetaceans, and especially birds, produce "songs" so rhythmically inventive and melodically complex that they put humankind to shame. Even the very elements of earth, air, fire, and water have their own tonal expression. Throughout time, musicians and composers have been inspired by the musical qualities of nature. Consider the aquatic impressionism of Debussy's "La Mer" or the tempestuous storm rendered in Beethoven's "Pastoral Symphony."

It is no accident that throughout the world, prayer is accompanied by song. The singing of hymns, the intoning of common notes by a congregation—these are ways of cutting through the veneer of everyday existence and tapping into a deeper spiritual place. Eastern meditative faiths, such as Buddhism and Hinduism, may begin prayer by sounding a bell or gong. And if you have ever experienced the calming resonance of a temple bowl, you know firsthand how the vibrations seem to seep into the soul. In India, it is said that the universe hangs on sound. This is not just any sound but an all-pervasive harmonic tone—so vast and subtle that it surrounds and informs all life.

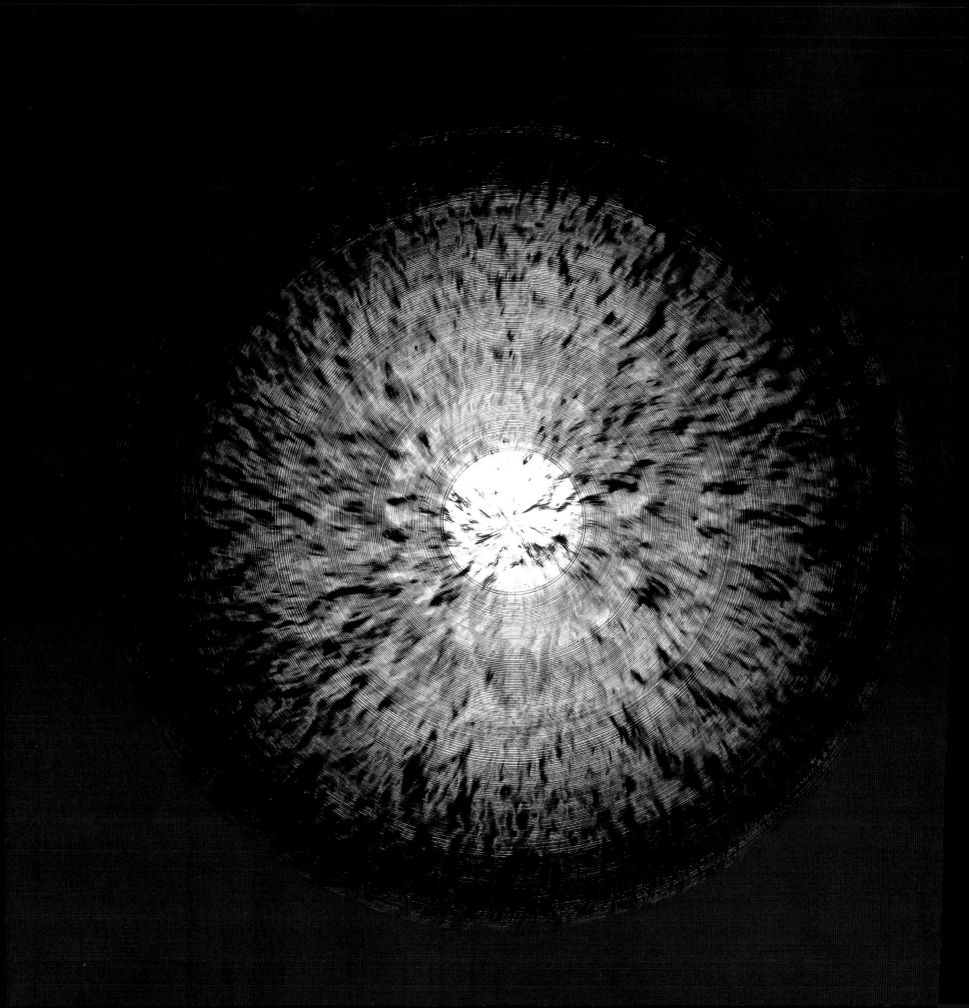

GONG

Mystery, spirituality, beauty, and power—all this can be found in the sound of a **Gong**.

Gongs are metal discs, often forged from bronze. Some have a flat surface, others have a rim that is turned inward. Button gongs have a raised, hill-like center. The gongs of East and Southeast Asia, particularly in China and Indonesia, vary greatly in size and tone. The sound of a fine gong matures as it ages, gaining a deeper and darker sound. It is said that the true voice of a gong will not be heard until thirty years have passed.

Historically, Asian gongs were a symbol of wealth and royalty; the greater the fortune, the larger the gong. Sometimes they were even used as currency. Similar to some African drums and to bells the world over, gongs were once used to send messages, sound alarms, call people to assembly, and announce deaths. Gongs were struck by armies to signal retreat. They were believed to banish evil spirits and attract wind or rain. It is said that to be touched by the sound of a gong imparts strength and happiness, and that "bathing" in the vibrations of a gong can restore health.

AMADINDA

n southern Uganda, some musicians of the Baganda tribe carry on a musical tradition dating back to the sixteenth century. They perform on a large xylophone called an **Amadinda** (*ah mah DIN dah*). This instrument averages five feet in length and three feet in width. It consists of twelve hardwood bars tied onto a wooden frame. In times past, the frame would have been temporary, constructed of newly cut banana stems.

The bars of an *amadinda* are usually hewn from the *lusambya* or *mukerembo* tree. These dense hardwoods give the instrument its signature tones. The bars are loosely tied to the frame, allowing them to resonate.

Traditionally, *amadinda* music is played by three percussionists seated at a single instrument. The music requires the musicians to play separate but interdependent rhythms. Patterns interlock, with each player striking a bar between the strokes of the others—one player's hand comes up as another player's hand goes down. This is a difficult drumming technique to master, especially at fast tempos. When it is done right, it is impossible to tell where one player stops and another begins. The resulting music is truly hypnotic.

MBIRA

Sansa, kalimba, luvale, karimba, marimbula, matape, **Mbira** (*im BEE rah*)—these are some of the names for instruments commonly known as "African thumb pianos." Metal or wooden tines are fastened to sound-boards of wood, steel, or gourd, and plucked by the player's thumbs and fingers. Shells, bottle caps, or beads are often attached to make the tines buzz when the instrument is played. *Mbiras* are frequently played inside large calabash gourds, which amplify the sound. And what a sound! *Mbira* music is water music. Zimbabwean musician Stella Chiweshe describes it as "tuned raindrops."

Some believe that each key of the *mbira* contains a spirit, such as father, grandfather, mother, or first child. As the keys are played, they grow hotter and sound sweeter until a given spirit is revealed as a memory, or a waking dream.

In Zimbabwe, there is a ceremony that combines singing, dancing, *mbira* playing, and home-brewed beer. The music can last all night, and in its most powerful moments may bring spirits into the ceremony. It is called a *bira* and is sometimes used by family members who seek the aid or advice of ancestral spirits. These spirits are summoned by particular *mbira* songs. If someone is sick in the mind or heart, or if their soul is tormented, the remedy may be *mbira*.

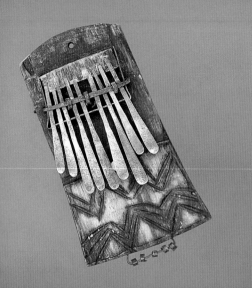

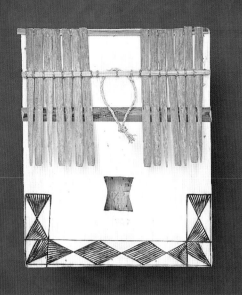

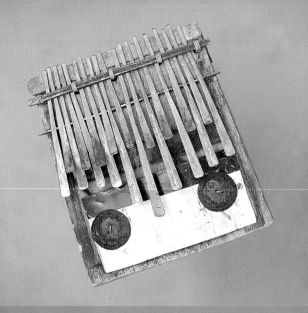

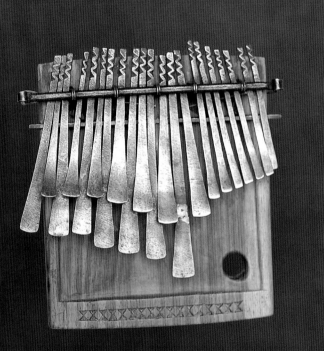

Clockwise from top left:

- **Luvale**, Zambia
- **Sansa**, Cameroon
- **Karimba**, Zimbabwe
- **Marimbula**, USA
- **Karimba**, Zimbabwe
- **Kalimba**, South Africa
- Name and origin unknown
- **Mbira**, Zimbabwe

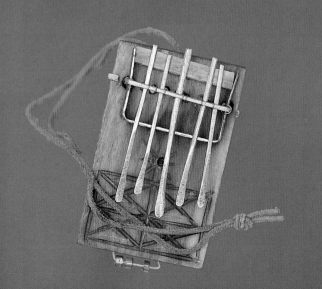

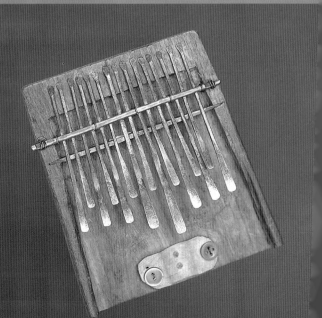

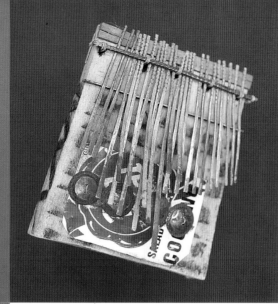

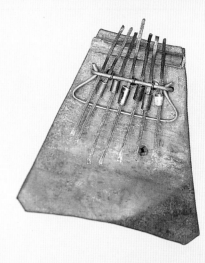

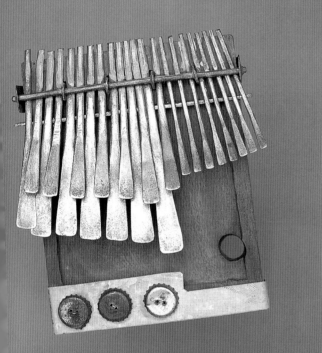

Clockwise from top left:

- **Karimba**, Zimbabwe
- **Matape**, Zimbabwe
- **Sansa**, Uganda
- **Karimba**, USA
- **Mbira**, Zimbabwe
- **Karimba**, Zimbabwe
- **Karimba**, Zimbabwe
- **Mbira**, Zimbabwe

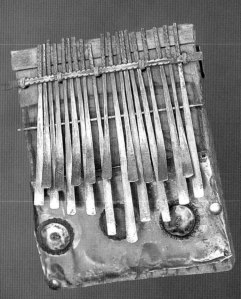

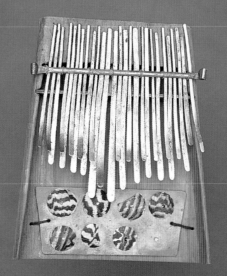

BALAFON

I n the West African country of Mali, there is an instrument of kings and commoners used to speak to this world and the next, called the **Balafon** (*BA la fon*). According to legend, the *balafon* was revealed in a dream to Sumanguru Kantey, a tenth-century Malian king of the Minianka people.

Among the Minianka, the *balafon* is used in all religious ceremonies that establish contact with the invisible world. . . . When the *balafon* and reed flute are played together, their tonal vibrations strongly affect creatures without an outer ear. Reptiles, including poisonous snakes, are called out of hiding and people wear shoes on such occasions to protect themselves. Traditional musicians will not play the *balafon* unless they are wearing protective amulets designed to repel any bad spirits among the many attracted by the music of this sacred instrument.

—Yaya Diallo, *The Healing Drum*

The *balafon* of today varies little from its tenth-century ancestors. Hardwood bars are cut and laid upon a frame. Gourd resonators are attached underneath to amplify the vibration of the bars. The gourds are pierced and the holes are covered, often with the fine, sticky webbing that spiders use to coat their eggs. When a bar is struck with a soft-ended mallet, these paper-thin coverings vibrate, creating a buzzing sound. *Balafon*s are played throughout West Africa and are sometimes called "gourd xylophones."

BERIMBAU

A curved stick, some wire, a gourd, a bit of string, a smaller stick, and a coin or stone—these are the components of a **Berimbau** (*bee rim BAU*). Add to that a little basket shaker filled with seeds or stones—the *caxixi*—and the magic begins.

To play a *berimbau*, the musician holds the curved stick in one hand. The other hand holds the small stick and the *caxixi*, striking the string that runs the length of the bow. The gourd resonator is opened and closed against the player's stomach. A coin or stone is used to change the pitch of the string, which sings and buzzes. The gourd "wah wahs," while the *caxixi* swirls and shakes.

The Brazilian *berimbau* is a descendant of African musical bows. Musical bows are some of the world's oldest known instruments. Cave paintings in the south of France, dating back to 15,000 B.C., depict people playing similar instruments. Today, musical bows are played in Africa, Cuba, and as far away as Guam, where they are called *mbilimbau*.

In Brazil, the *berimbau* found its core expression in the musical accompaniment of *capoeira*. *Capoeira* is difficult to define. It is a unique art form that combines martial arts, dance, music, and acrobatics. For true *capoeiristas*, however, it is more than this—it is a way of life.

Capoeira was created by African slaves in Brazil. Brazilian percussionist Airto Moreira describes it in the following passage from Mickey Hart's *Drumming at the Edge of Magic*:

> The *berimbau*, you know, was used in the slaves' martial art, *capoeira*. The slaves were not allowed to practice *capoeira* openly or it would have seemed to the plantation guards that they were practicing for war. So while they fought they played the *berimbau* in a particular rhythm and whenever anyone spotted a guard the rhythm would change and everyone would start dancing. The guard would come and look and say, "Oh, good. The slaves are happy. So let's leave 'em alone, let's get out of here." As soon as they were gone the rhythm of the *berimbau* would change and they'd start fighting or training again.

The *berimbau* is still used to accompany *capoeira* today, but thanks to Brazilian musicians Moreira, Nana Vasconcelos, Dom um Romão, and others, this unique instrument has also found its way into jazz, pop, and other contemporary music.

STEEL PAN

From the twin-island nation of Trinidad and Tobago comes the **Steel Pan**. The first pan orchestras were very different from the steel bands we hear today. The musicians played garbage can lids, biscuit tins, milk cans, and dustpans that they wore around their necks. Then someone discovered that if you hammered these homemade metal instruments, making hills and valleys, they would produce clear and distinct pitches.

During World War II, when refineries on the islands began to discard their 55-gallon oil drums, the nascent instrument makers took what they had learned from making smaller instruments to forge the first steel drums. As their technique developed, they were able to craft special pans for playing melody, harmony, and bass or rhythm.

It is hard to believe, but once the sweet sound of steel pans was considered outlaw music because of the violence that erupted when rival bands met. Island legislators restricted the use of pans to the slums. In these "panyards," musicians could only play at designated times, thus forcing the music to go underground. The image of steel bands changed in the 1950s, coinciding with a rise in tourism. Today, young people are encouraged to join steel bands and, in 1995, the once-renegade steel pan was officially declared the national instrument of Trinidad and Tobago.

TO MAKE A STEEL PAN

To make a steel pan, use a sledgehammer to sink the closed end of an oil drum. Cut the drum to the desired depth. Draw circles with chalk to define the positions of the notes. Then use a smaller hammer to beat out each position. To finish, temper the surface with fire and water.

GAMELAN

t is an orchestra of bronze, the musical interplay of opposites: shadow and light, quiet and storm—this is the **Gamelan** (*GAM ah lahn*) of Indonesia.

A gamelan is an ensemble of tuned percussion including gongs, cymbals, drums, xylophones, and metallophones (xylophone-like instruments with metal bars). A full ensemble may also include bamboo flutes, fiddles, zithers, and male and female vocalists. This most communal of ensembles has no formal conductor. Instead, changes in tempo and intensity are signaled by a drummer from the center of the group.

Gamelan music is full of color, nuance, and detail. It is associated with the poetry, dance, and theater of the Indonesian islands of Java and Bali. In Java, the music is ringing and meditative. Balinese gamelan is often more raucous, filled with shimmering, rhythmic patterns. Javanese gamelan accompanies *wayang kulit*, a shadow puppet theater that sometimes lasts all night. Gamelan players also perform at social functions such as temple festivals, funerals, and weddings. In fact, there is an old Javanese saying: "It is not official until the gong is hung."

There are gamelans of bamboo, iron, and even aluminum, but the classic voice is of bronze. Spreading out from Indonesia, a great diversity of gamelans and gamelan styles are played today, entrancing audiences throughout the world.

The *gender*, pictured opposite, is one of the metallophones of the gamelan. During a performance of *wayang kulit*, the *gender* is played constantly, accompanying and elaborating on the voice of the shadow puppeteer.

BAMBOO ANGKLUNG

Y ou are walking through a village in West Java. Bicycles fill the streets and the air is a banquet of scents—peanuts roasting, spices, teas, and clove cigarettes. Out of one boombox pours frenetic rhythms sounding like "dang-dut, dang-dut, dang-dut." It is the sound of Indonesian pop music, aptly named...*dangdut*. From another radio, you hear Michael Jackson. In the midst of this chaos, you notice something different—melodious and conversational. You follow your ears to an open pavilion. Inside, a group of men are seated in a circle, trading notes upon an instrument called a **Bamboo Angklung** (*AHNG klung*).

Each segment of this instrument is a kind of rattle, with two or three bamboo tubes suspended in series on a wooden frame. The tubes are tuned in octaves. When shaken, they produce a dry, hollow, yet singing tone—like a combination of a xylophone and bamboo wind chimes. The bamboo *angklung* is commonly played in an ensemble, sometimes with as many as twenty-seven players. The rattles are held in each player's hands and notes are traded back and forth in a manner similiar to that of a Western hand bell choir.

In Bali, there is a bamboo orchestra called *gamelan jegog*. The bass instruments alone are ten feet in length and the players straddle them like jockeys on racehorses. The rumble can be heard from a great distance.

TRIANGLE

The **Triangle** is musical geometry—its shape is its name. It is made by bending a steel bar into an isosceles or equilateral triangle, leaving one corner open. The pitch of a triangle seems indeterminate when played alone but, like a chameleon, it adapts to the primary tonality of its surroundings. While usually small in size, the triangle's sound is piercing and its many harmonic overtones can be heard over an entire orchestra. Classical European composers such as Liszt, Grieg, and Wagner have employed its ringing voice to powerful effect.

Although its form is simple, the triangle is not always easy to play. With technique and practice, the player creates rapid, subtle rhythms by striking an interior angle between two bars with a metal beater. One can hear this playing style in Cajun and zydeco music from the state of Louisiana and in the samba music of Brazil.

Large triangles with sides up to two feet in length were once used on North American farms and ranches to sound the alarm in emergencies. They were also played to call workers in from the fields at meal times. These utilitarian triangles were called "dinner bells" or "chow irons."

In Louisiana, there is a Cajun triangle known as a *tee fer* ("little iron") or *bastringue*. It is made from the spring-steeled teeth of old horse-drawn hay rakes. The open ends of the triangle are curled to lower the pitch, giving the *tee fer* its distinctive sound and shape. Sadly, its days of production may be numbered since the old hay rakes have not been manufactured since the 1940s.

BELLS

The world is filled with the sound of **Bells**. Their voices are a marriage of magic and utility. Over the centuries, the tasks they perform have ranged from the mundane to the cosmic. They call us to worship, celebrate our weddings, mourn our deaths, herald the coronations of monarchs, keep track of stray livestock, signal someone at the door or on the telephone, and mark time on a ship, in a school, or at a boxing match.

Edgar Allan Poe was fascinated by the musical eloquence of bells. In his poem "The Bells," Poe describes some of their voices and moods:

> Hear the sledges with the bells—
> Silver bells!
> *What* a world of merriment their melody foretells!
> How they tinkle, tinkle, tinkle,
> In the icy air of night!
> While the stars that oversprinkle
> All the Heavens, seem to twinkle
> With a crystalline delight....

Whether formed from goat horn, wood, or the more familiar metals, the shape and substance of bells are as varied as the sounds they contain. Bells ring, ching, ding, jingle, jangle, tinkle, clang, chime, clamor, peal, knell—and toll.

LEARNING TO PLAY
GHANAIAN BELLS

When I began my study of Ghanaian drumming, I spent a long time playing *gankogui* (double bell) and rarely was allowed to play a drum. At first I found this demeaning. After all, I was a drummer. It was especially embarrassing when I would "lose" my bell part during a rehearsal. My teacher would play out the pattern on my head! I soon realized that these seemingly simple bell patterns were quite difficult to play correctly.

Finally, the day came when we fledgling drummers fit our different bell patterns together for the first time. The effect was almost dizzying; the interplay of rhythm and melody was wonderful! The tones of the different bells beat against each other, creating melodies that no one was even playing. I became so excited that I lost my part and, quick as a wink, felt the rhythmic rap-rap-rap of my teacher's knuckles on my head!

⊢ **Tingcha,**
Nepal

⊤
Larger Almglocken,
Switzerland

Smaller Almglocken,
Germany

Prayer Bell, ⊣
Japan

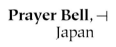

Sarna Bells,
India
⊥

⊢ **Cowbell, Ago-go,**
Brazil

Chime Tree, ⊣
India

Masai Goat Bell, ⊣
Kenya

Wooden Bell,
Thailand

⊤
Elephant Bell,
Burma

⊢ **Bini Ceremonial Bell,**
Nigeria

TEMPLE BOWL

Coolness and purity describe the transcendent sound of a "singing bowl" or **Temple Bowl**. This instrument of meditation and contemplation is used to accompany Confucian hymns and Buddhist chants. The Chinese temple bowl (or bell) *pu-chung* is struck at the beginning of a chanted phrase to establish the proper pitch and mood.

Temple bowls and temple bells date back to the earliest days of Confucianism and Buddhism. The oldest known Japanese *dobachi* is attributed to A.D. 646. The *dobachi*, which is made from hammered bronze, rests on a padded ring and is struck with an upward motion. Its incredibly clear tone resonates for a very long time.

Some temple bowls are made to "sing" by rubbing a stick around the rim, not unlike rubbing a moistened finger around the edge of a wine glass. The resulting sound is otherworldly.

"... If we trust the true and sure words written in Indian leaves, we will hear all past and future in one stroke of the temple bell."

—Li Shang-Yin
(A.D. 812–858)

DRUMS

As music or as metaphor, drums have inspired, vexed, seduced, enraptured, and enlightened us. Poet Walt Whitman heard a solemn funeral song in the measured cadence of military drums. Composer Duke Ellington proclaimed "a drum is a woman," and created an inspired jazz suite of the same name to illustrate his point. Novelist Oscar Hijuelos conjured the poetic voices of drums in his book *The Mambo Kings Play Songs of Love*:

> . . . the beating-of-a-pillow drums, heavy-stones-against-a-wall drums, then the-thickest-forest-tree-trunks-pounding drums, and then the-mountain-rumble drums, the-little-birds-learning-to-fly drums. . . .

The multitude and variety of drums is staggering. Consider their shapes: hourglass, cylindrical, goblet, barrel, cone, footed, or framed. They are fashioned from just about any material imaginable: clay, wood, bamboo, gourd, metal, plastic, and fiberglass. The *damaru*, a Tibetan drum, is in fact made from human skulls. Drums are struck, of course, but they also can be tapped, snapped, brushed, and rubbed. They shout, then whisper—telling secrets. Drums rustle, ripple, march, dance, bend, and buzz. Drums laugh, but can also give voice to tears. They are the life of the party, a carnival strut, the slow burial pulse, and a blues tattoo.

Even in the absence of deliberately crafted instruments, drumming still occurs. As musical essayist W. A. Mathieu observed: "The body is the first drum. Less obvious are tabletops, ladder rungs, car roofs. . . ."

SLIT DRUM

It is impossible to know how rhythm and music began. Those first vibrations leave no archaeological traces. But we do know that one of the oldest instruments is the "log" or **Slit Drum**. Slit drums were first made from hollowed trees. The playing surface of the drum was slit to create two or more notes and was struck with sticks. In some African cultures, a language of the slit drum developed, using variations of rhythm, pitch, and intensity. The largest and most resonant of these drums were used to send messages across great distances. This means of communication was sometimes called the "African telegraph."

Some [African] slit drums are given proper names usually consisting of a proverb, symbol or riddle: "Pain doesn't kill," "Death has no master," "The river always flows in its bed," "Birds don't steal from empty fields,". . . . The real purpose of these names is not just to identify the instrument, but also to confer upon it the virtues that they describe or to remind the musician and his neighbors of the truths and moral precepts on which everyday actions should be based.

—Francis Bebey, *African Music: A People's Art*

Slit drums were also common to parts of Asia, the Pacific Rim, and the Americas. Centuries ago, the Aztecs crafted decorative slit drums called *teponaxtles*. These were sacred drums, each with a specific ceremonial role. Some were played during harvest festivals, others during weddings or funerals. One special slit drum was only heard at the annual festival honoring the ancient king Tepozteco, who, according to Aztec legend, was the inventor of this instrument.

In another part of the world, the Naga people of India carved an intricately ornamented slit drum that was fifty feet long! Such was the importance of this huge drum that the people built a special dwelling just to house it.

The popular wooden tongue drums found in gift shops and music stores today continue the lineage of slit drums into the present.

TALKING DRUM

They are called *chang-go* in Korea. Ghanaians call them *luna*. In India, they go by the name of *udukkai*; in Senegal, *tama*. All indicate a squeeze, pressure, or **Talking Drum** and share these characteristics: an hourglass shape, a head on the top and bottom, and strings or cords connecting both heads.

In West Africa, the talking drum is held between the upper arm and left side of the body, while simultaneously squeezing and striking the drum with a curved stick. The pitches shift with every squeeze and release, creating singing rhythms and a gliding, conversational sound. In the hands of a master, the talking drum "speaks" in many ways—mimicking human speech, answering a singer, telling jokes and stories, singing poems of praise, or just playing music.

The Dagbamba people of Ghana created a precise talking drum vocabulary based on the tonal qualities of their spoken language. They use the voice of the *luna* as that of a troubadour or scribe. Rhythms played on *lunas* without knowledge of this drum language are scorned by master drummers as "nonsense music." Sadly, the drum languages of many societies are being lost as the electronic world of telephones, televisions, radios, and computers takes over the esteemed role of communication once held by the drum.

TALK: TO ARTICULATE. TO IMITAT

TO CONVEY ONE'S THOUGHTS IN A WA

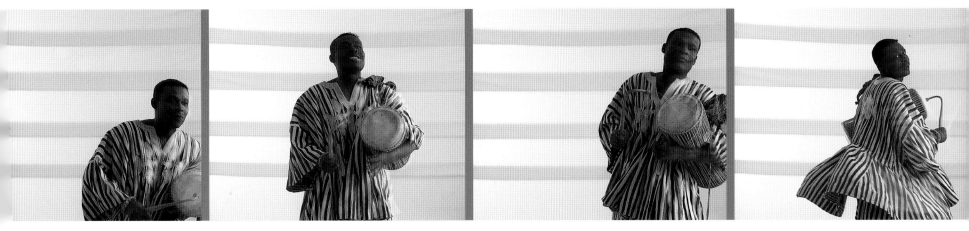

THE SOUNDS OF HUMAN SPEECH.

OTHER THAN BY SPOKEN WORDS.

TABLA

There are many kinds of drums in India. Perhaps the best known is the **Tabla** (*tah bla*). Hindu legend attributes its creation to the god Shiva. In the story "Shiva and the Ash Demon," from her collection *Patakin*, Nina Jaffe tells of the birth of the tabla. In a trance, Shiva flies out of his body and comes to the edge of the Indian Ocean:

> There, floating upon the beach, was a *coco de mer*, a sea coconut—the rare fruit that washes up onto the shores of India all the way from Madagascar. Shiva picked up the sea coconut, and with the flame of his third eye he sliced it in half. He covered each half with skin from the snakes that encircled his body, and began to play. From the drum on his right there came the sound of birds singing, of brooks bubbling, of leaves rustling in the breeze. All the creatures of the world stopped to hear his music. And when he struck the drum on the left, there came the sound of the earth shaking, of booming thunder, of trees crackling in a storm. And this was the very first tabla drum.

Tabla consists of a pair of drums played by one drummer, the *tablaji*. The *bhaya*, the lower-pitched drum, is made with a metal shell. The tabla, the higher-pitched drum, is made with a wooden shell. Each drum has a single head comprised of three skins and finished with a circle of black paste in the center. The finger drumming style of the tabla is highly refined and can be accomplished only after years of study.

Tabla, the rhythmic heart of northern Indian classical music, is often heard in ensemble with the sitar and the tamboura.

Many of the tabla's dazzling playing techniques originated with older Indian drums, such as the twin-headed *mridangam* (below) of southern India and the *pakhawaj* of the north.

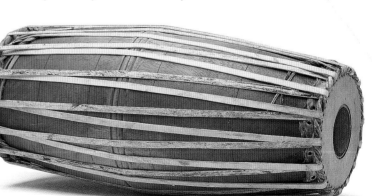

AMERICAN INDIAN DRUMS

Frame drums, shakers, water-filled kettle-like drums, large and small double-headed drums, and leg and ankle rattles all serve as the rhythmic accompaniment for the human voice—the essential instrument in much American Indian music. Descendants of some five hundred nations, American Indian tribes each have their own customs and beliefs. What their many drums symbolize and share is an abiding respect for the past, a strong sense of family and community, and a reverence for all living things.

Wherever American Indian music is played—in concert, at a pow wow, or at a tribal ceremony—radiating from the center is the rhythm of the heartbeat. Unlike the polyrhythms of other cultures, the emphasis here is on playing in unison, blending individual rhythms into a single communal pulse. Similar to some African societies that have no separate name for music and dance, **American Indian Drums** and voices are usually combined and simply called "singing."

Before the cedar and horsehide drum pictured here could be used for the first time, four songs were sung into it. This is a traditional way of honoring the warrior spirit, a practice that reaches back generations. In this case, the songs represented the four branches of the United States armed forces. Now the drum can be a proper home to the songs of the grandfathers who live inside it.

DJEMBE

An African hand drum rapidly growing in popularity worldwide is the **Djembe** (*JEM bay*). In the North African country of Mali, it is carved from a tree trunk into a goblet or vase shape. It is tapered this way to fit between a drummer's legs, while the body of the instrument is suspended from straps across the drummer's shoulders.

Traditionally, the *djembe* has a goathide or other animal skin drum head that is tuned with ropes. Sometimes small metal plates with steel rattles or shells are inserted into the *djembe's* tuning ropes. The plates buzz and rattle sympathetically when the drum is struck.

Djembes have spread throughout the world in a diaspora of percussion, inspiring new combinations of shells, skins, tuning styles, and playing techniques. Although it has many voices, three deceptively simple strokes identify the sound of the *djembe*, each of which may take a year or more to master. The drum's lightning-like crack electrifies its listeners. Its crisp middle range carries the rhythm, while its deep bass voice seems to ascend from the earth itself. It is said that in the right hands, the *djembe* even has the power to heal.

THE POWER OF THE DJEMBE

Let me tell you a story:

I was giving a performance in a primary school in Illinois and I began with the music of the *djembe*.

There was something special happening from the start. The acoustics of the room amplified every stroke with great clarity. When I played a flurry of notes, "ghost" tones seemed to suspend in the air.

I began slowly, introducing the softer voices of the drum. As the rhythms began building, the groove established—then deepened. Like a trio of drums, the rich bass notes tied with the shaker-like brushing strokes and higher slapping commentary. My hands began to fly and I found myself in a rare place—in control and yet not in control.

The room had the same feeling of suspension as that of a baseball game before a decisive pitch: at once strangely calm, yet completely charged. The roll of the drum seemed to build emotionally almost of its own doing—louder, louder . . . louder still. I stopped. Nothing. Silence.

Then came a scream—not of fright or shock, but full of joy. Ecstatic, like a long-suppressed secret finally being told.

Everyone in the room froze for a moment, including me. Then I felt a need to bring things back into control, so I continued with the program. The rest went as it usually does, with no big surprises.

After the performance, one of the teachers approached me. She had clearly been crying and quietly explained what had happened. The outburst was from one of her third-grade students, a girl. This student was autistic and no one in the school had ever heard her voice.

CONGA

The **Conga** (*CUNG ga*) has found a place in rock bands, country and western groups, symphony orchestras, jazz combos, and popular bands from Africa to South America. Yet its highest expression may be found in the explosive Latin music called salsa.

Congas can be divided into three groups: the *quinto*, which is the smallest and highest-pitched drum, the middle-range conga, and the large *tumbadora*. Played by a master *conguero* these drums have infinite possibilities. The drummer's strokes dart and weave, like a boxer's hands. Lifting the drums up with the knees changes the tone and pitch. A rubbed finger makes the conga moan. And when a hand comes cracking down—like a slap in the face—the conga shouts!

The congas we hear today are hybrids of the Congolese drums brought to the Americas by African slaves. Plantation owners sensed the power of the drums and banned them. But the sound of hands on hides would not be silenced, and—along with other drums such as the *bata* and bongos—congas provided the rhythm of rebellion. These rhythms are the foundation of modern Latin music. Drummers gather in parks from Havana to New York City, where the sound of their congas echoes off sidewalks and graffiti-covered walls. Secreted in their Afro-Latin rhythms we hear the whisper of history.

BONGOS

n the United States, the 1950s were a time of coffeehouses, beatniks, hip slang—"like cool, daddy-o"—and poets in jeans and turtlenecks reciting "beat poetry." The beat for this Beat Generation was often provided by a pair of **Bongos** (*BAHN goz*).

Bongos are small double drums, traditionally played between a seated drummer's legs. In Latin bands, the *bongosero* plays a set of wooden bongos with calfskin heads that are usually tuned a fourth apart. While the congas, maracas, cowbells, and *clavés* lay down the groove, the high-pitched bongos chatter on top, providing cross rhythms and counterpoint. Although diminutive in size, under knowing hands they are capable of complexity, subtlety, and power.

Bongo-like twin drums can be found in India and Pakistan as well as many African countries. In Morocco, they are called *tebilat* and their thick shells, made from heavy porcelain, are often decoratively painted.

DOUMBEK

One discovers a vast world of Arabic percussion throughout the Middle East: small cymbals, wooden and metal spoons, castanets, tambourines, frame drums, and the hand drum known as the **Doumbek** (*DOOM bek*).

As you cross the many borders of land and language in this region, the *doumbek*'s name and spelling varies—*darabouka, darbukah, demblik, dümbelek, dumbek*—but all identify a goblet-shaped hand drum with a clay, wooden, or engraved metal shell and a single drum head. The drum usually rests horizontally across the player's lap and is struck with the fingers and open palm of the hand. The *doumbek* is a drum of great range. In fact, the word *doumbek* is derived from *doum* or *dum*, which refers to the instrument's surprisingly deep bass tones, and *bek*, which names its crisp treble voice. The pitch can be fluidly raised or lowered by inserting and removing a fist through the open end of the drum's shell while playing.

Doumbeks can be heard in much of the Islamic world. They are equally at home in the devotional songs of a Cairo wedding or the pulsing *rai* music of a Moroccan discotheque. From market to minaret, their rhythms dance.

FRAME DRUMS

Frame Drums are simplicity itself: a skin fastened and stretched across a hoop to create an instrument with a diameter greater than its depth. Though some are square or multisided, most frame drums are circular. It is not by coincidence that most of the world's drums involve circles. Whether as a symbol of wholeness and completion or as a centerpoint, the powerful geometry of the circle has a resonance that is social and symbolic as well as musical. There is also a practical consideration, since a circular drum is the easiest to tune.

Pakistan, India, Italy, Ireland, Brazil, many Asian countries, the North American West, and the Middle East possess long traditions of frame drumming. Frame drums go by many names: *tar, duff, def, xinjiang, doyre,* and *kanjira,* to name but a few. For centuries the frame drummers of Arab lands were primarily women. In fact, a Hebrew name for the frame drum is *tuf miryam,* meaning "Miriam's drum." In Morocco, a few strands of animal gut or nylon are stretched across the undersurface of a frame drum head to create the snare-like *bendir.* In Egypt, large jingles are pinned into intricately inlaid frames to make a *riq,* yet another variation of the familiar frame drums we call tambourines.

TAMBOURINES

Tambourines!
Tambourines!
Tambourines
To the glory of God!
Tambourines
To glory!

A gospel shout
And a gospel song;
Life is short
But God is long!

Tambourines!
Tambourines!
Tambourines
To glory!

—Langston Hughes

TAMBOURINE

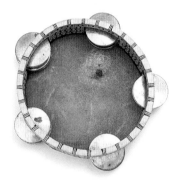

The **Tambourine** has come through the centuries relatively unchanged. Although there are variations in shape, size, and construction, the tambourine remains a frame drum with jingles suspended from pins along openings on the frame. From such a simple instrument, amazing playing styles have evolved. Middle Eastern *riq* players use a variety of drumming techniques: striking with the palm, fingertips, or knuckles; shaking; finger snapping on the rim; brushing and flicking the jingles; bouncing the *riq* between knee and hand; and using the friction of a moistened thumb to create "thumb rolls." In Brazil, where they play a tambourine called a *pandeiro*, players also spin and throw the instrument into the air with eye-popping dexterity.

I first encountered virtuoso tambourine playing in an American Baptist church. Although a number of singers in the choir played tambourines, one woman really stood out. When the music started to rock, her playing went into double time. The tambourine seemed to fly, hand to knee to elbow into the air and back again, effortlessly and in perfect rhythm, never missing a beat. She executed thumb rolls, ending them with a slap that sounded like a thunderclap. Fluttering thumb and fingertip rolls followed, rising and falling like an ocean tide. Her tambourine danced as if possessed by a spirit—which, of course, it was.

> **"When Pharoah's horses, chariots, and horsemen went into the sea, the Lord brought the waters of the sea back over them, but the Israelites walked through the sea on dry ground. Then Miriam the prophetess, Aaron's sister, took a tambourine in her hand, and all the women followed her, with tambourines and dancing."**
>
> **—Exodus 15:24**

BODHRAN

The **Bodhran** (*bah rahn*) is a frame drum from Ireland. It has a goatskin head and is usually reinforced from the inside with a crossbar. What distinguishes this drum from other frame drums is not its construction, but the manner in which it is played. Traditionally, it was played with the hands, but currently a more pervasive playing style is to use one hand on the inside of the drum with the other holding a small, two-headed wooden beater called a pin, or tipper. The pin is held like a pencil and its strokes move up and down from the wrist, like shaking water from the hand. When perfected, this technique creates a wonderful rolling kind of rhythm, ideally suited for accompanying other Irish folk instruments, such as the tin whistle or the fiddle. And boy, does it dance!

The *bodhran* dates back at least four centuries. Its place in Irish history is ceremonial as well as musical. To celebrate St. Stephen's Day, which is the night after Christmas, children went from house to house asking for money to pay for the burial of a small bird. This was called the "hunt for the wren." The children were accompanied by mummers (costumed actors) and musicians, including *bodhran* players. After the ceremony, the *bodhrans* were destroyed.

The *bodhran*'s thumping, rolling sound, heard in a variety of contemporary music, is still most at home with traditional Irish folk music where, like a Celtic heartbeat, it harkens back to its Druid roots.

HOW A BODHRAN IS MADE

Nina Jaffe describes how to make a *bodhran* in her book, *Patakin*:

"There is a special art to making a *bodhran*. The drum makers who still practice their craft keep the family secrets closely guarded. The drum maker will choose a goatskin just the right strength, just the right thickness, and then bury it in the ground. He might leave it in for one week, or for two or more—that is his own secret. After the skin has been softened in the earth, it will be wrapped around a hoop made from barrel staves."

TAIKO

Beneath the neon surface of modern Japanese life, there is a reverence for traditional arts and religious customs. The sounds of percussion play an important role in both. Shinto monks mark prayer intervals by sounding a huge *moku-gyo* (Japanese for "wooden fish"). Gongs are intoned in Buddhist temples and *gagaku* orchestras. Bells, woodblocks, bamboo castanets, clappers, and many types of drums accompany the ancient dramas of Noh and Kabuki.

Taiko (*TIGH ko*) is one of the most respected and powerful of all Japanese drums. It is a wooden, barrel-shaped drum with animal skins nailed to both ends of its shell. The *taiko* is played with large sticks called *bachi*, using drumming techniques traditional to Shinto and Buddhist practice. *Taiko* drumming is often highly stylized and choreographed, owing nearly as much to theater and dance as it does to music.

In the past, enormous *taiko* were used to set village boundaries. If you could hear the drumming of the *taiko*, you were still within the village lands. In rural districts, villagers sometimes used *taiko* and other drums to drive away evil spirits. Some believed that the playing of drums and gongs during an eclipse of the sun would force it to reappear.

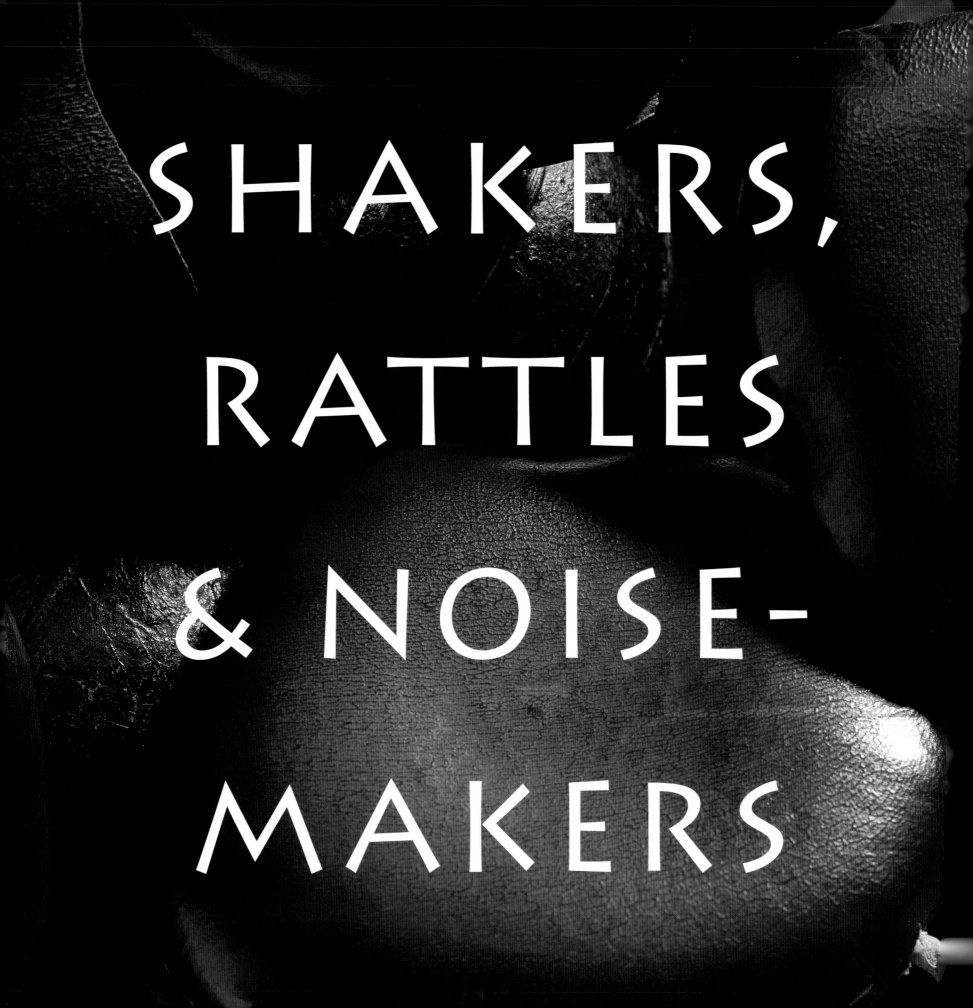

usical instruments are commonly divided into four sections: strings, brass, woodwinds, and percussion. Early in the twentieth century, musicologists Curt Sachs and Erich M. von Hornbostel developed a different way of classifying instruments. Their system, which is similar to one employed in India, established four broad categories: aerophones (instruments that produce sound by using air or breath), chordophones (stringed instruments), membranophones (drums with stretched heads), and idiophones (instruments that produce sound through the vibration of a solid material). Idiophones are a large and eclectic group ranging from anvils to woodblocks. Included in this group are tuned instruments, such as xylophones, and untuned instruments such as shakers, rattles, and noisemakers.

Whether fabricated from cocopods or cocoons, bamboo or the jawbone of a donkey, these instruments are all drawn from the bountiful realms of nature. In Mexico, a gourd or a cow's horn is notched to become a scraper called the *guiro*. Domino-sized pieces of wood are tied in sequence to create a Japanese *bin-sasara* with its locust-like sound. American Indians fashion rattles from deerskin, antelope horn, turtle shell, and elm bark. And on the Jewish holiday of Purim, we hear the wooden clatter of the *gregor,* an Eastern European ratchet. The simplicity of all these instruments can be deceptive. In the right hands, shakers are capable of very complex and challenging playing styles. Other noisemakers require little or no learned technique—anyone can make one, everyone can play.

Since ancient times, these elemental instruments have been imbued with magical power and symbolism. These are the village cleansers as well as the party favors, the animal scarers, and the spirit magnets. They are relied on to heal or haunt, celebrate or mourn, and are at the crossroads of music and noise.

RAINSTICK

Something in all of us seeks out the natural world. This is as true for a farmer in Peru as it is for an oceanographer in Los Angeles. In the autumn leaves crunching beneath our feet and the whispering of tall grass in the wind, we hear a quality akin to music. So it is with the sound of rain. Rain comes in sheets, sprinkles, showers, and storms. Across the world, people have created instruments to imitate its many voices.

There is a Chilean legend that **Rainsticks** were created to remind the spirits that rain was needed. In Central and South America, rainsticks are made from cactus, woven baskets, or gourds. In Africa, slender termite-hollowed trees are used; in Asia, bamboo. The design is almost always the same—a tube, with thorns or nails driven through it, filled with seeds, shells, lava pebbles, or stones. When the tube is inverted, the pellets cascade down, recreating the magical sound of rain.

RHYTHM STICKS

Pu-ili sticks, also known as "Filipino buzz sticks" or "devil chasers," are **Rhythm Sticks** made from tubes of split bamboo. They can be shaken like a switch or a rattle, struck together, or played against the body, producing an insect-like buzzing sound. Variants of this instrument are found throughout Oceania and in other areas where bamboo is common. In Polynesia, *pu-ili* sticks are played by dancers and used in hula orchestras.

Some of the rhythm sticks used by the Aborigines of Australia are beautifully carved with intricate designs. The patterns are echoed in Aboriginal art and stories of mythic beings who wandered the land in the time of creation, called "the Dreamtime." These beings crossed the continent singing out the names of everything—sandhills, watering holes, trees, insects, animals—and thus "sang the world into being." They also left trails of music called "songlines" in their wake. Songlines are the source of most traditional Aboriginal music. These songs are often accompanied by body percussion such as clapping and foot stamping, the drumming together of boomerangs, and the playing of rhythm sticks called *bilma* (pictured below).

Clavés are at the heart of much Latin American music. They are two resonant hardwood sticks. One is perched in a cupped hand to increase the volume, while the other is struck against it. Their piercing voice cuts through even the loudest salsa band.

BULLROARER

A flat piece of wood, metal, or bone is swung by a string over the player's head. The air passing over and around the object causes it to vibrate, and out comes the sound—a deep whir. One person hears it as voices, another as the drone of an enormous insect, yet another hears the deep-throated growl of an animal. Such is the enigmatic character of the **Bullroarer**.

In some cultures the bullroarer is a sacred object used as a kind of "spirit broom" to ritually cleanse a village. It may be played over the deceased at a funeral ceremony or whirled to scare away wild animals.

Bullroarers are found throughout the world, and their varied names sound like music—*luvuvu, tangalop, riwi-riwi loco, goingoing, oupa, mbirimbiri,* and *epop*. But by whatever name, the bullroarer's howl evokes its ancient past and stirs our imagination.

SISTRUM

The **Sistrum** (*SIS trum*), an ancient handheld rattle, has a recorded history that dates back to 2500 B.C. It takes its name from the Greek *seistron*, meaning "thing shaken." In *Percussion Instruments and Their History*, historian James Blades tells us:

The instrument is found in several forms, the earliest evidence of which may be found in the shark rattle preserved by Malayan and Melanesian fisherman, an implement consisting of a framework of rattan bent in the shape of a two-pronged fork or a tennis racket, strung with loose disks of coconut shell. In Japan, the *sistrum* is employed in Shinto worship. In parts of Abyssinia, the *sistrum* under the name of *tsanatsel* is still used by priests. A fork-shaped rattle resembling the implement preserved by Malayan fisherman is used by the Eskimos to entice seals.

Evidence of the *sistrum* has been discovered in Egypt, as well as in Sumaria and Babylonia. In ancient Egypt, these instruments may have been played primarily by women, but there is disagreement among historians about whether they were used in religious ceremonies or on occasions of a more salacious nature. The Greek and Roman empires spread the *sistrum*'s voice throughout the world, and variations can now be found in North and South America, Africa, and Asia.

Still heard today in ceremonies performed in the Ethiopian Coptic Christian Church, the *sistrum* accompanies songs of worship, just as its ancestors did so many centuries ago.

ANKLE RATTLES

When we think of percussion, we usually imagine hands—hands that clap, shake, strike, or rub an instrument. But percussion is not limited to the hand's domain. For those of us brought up in Western culture, percussion may bring to mind a drum set played with hands and feet: one foot for the bass drum, the other for the high-hat cymbals.

Another form of drumming with the feet is dancing. Consider the driving unison beat of clogging, the fiery rhythms of flamenco, the intricacies of classical Indian dance, and the jazz inflections of tap. Leg and **Ankle Rattles** bring another dimension to dance, one that is both percussive and ornamental. The sound of ankle rattles parallels the motions of the wearer, adding rhythm and texture, blurring the division between music and dance.

These wearable instruments, fashioned from cocoons, seedpods, animal hooves, bells, or other materials, are common to many cultures and are worn by shamans and medicine men as well as dancers and musicians.

MARACAS & OTHER SHAKERS

Across the globe we find a multitude of shakers and maraca-like instruments. Each is a musical world unto itself, with its own intrinsic techniques and qualities. **Maracas** are among the best known and least appreciated of percussion instruments. Often the last-minute mementos of a sunny vacation, they are taken about as seriously as a paper umbrella from a tropical drink. This misperception vanishes completely upon hearing virtuoso maraca playing.

A fine pair of maracas has a natural, balanced feel in the hands and sounds clear and precise. Each pair has a high- and low-pitched maraca, termed female and male respectively. Maracas can be played in a number of ways and are capable of rhythms as sophisticated and complex as those of a snare drum.

In Venezuela there is a folk music called *joropo* that tells stories of horsemen and life on the plains. In this music, maracas not only provide the rhythm, but are often featured as solo instruments. The basic playing technique utilizes a full motion of the body, including "rolls" that start behind the player's back and are whipped to the front. Many of these maraca patterns are derived from such activities as lassoing livestock and bronco riding.

The maracas pictured here are the handmade creations of Venezuelan Maximo B. Teppa. The yellowish gourds are called *tapara* and are filled with dried seeds. For a distinctly different sound, Teppa sometimes uses coconuts and fills his maracas with dried frog's eggs!

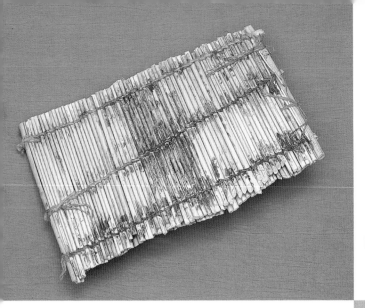

⊢ **Kayamba,**
Tanzania

⊤
Calabash Rattles,
Kenya

Wai Wai Maracá,
Brazil

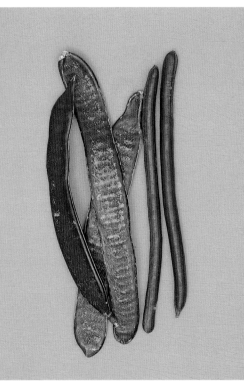

Seedpods, ⊣
Mexico

Hosho,
Zimbabwe
⊥

⊢ **Caxixi,**
Brazil

**Single and Double
Basket Shakers,**
Cameroon

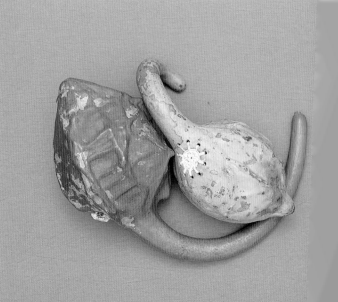

Flowershaker, ⊣
India

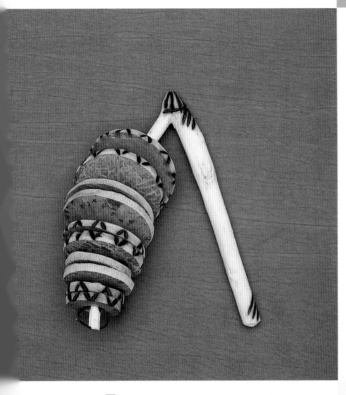

⊤
Sennpo,
Ivory Coast

Small Shekeres, ⊣
Ghana

Large Shekere,
Nigeria

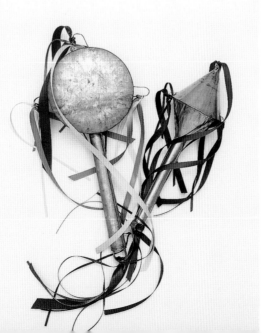

⊢ **Maracás,**
Brazil

FRATTOIR

Since the 1900s, scrub boards made of wood and steel have been used as percussion instruments in the folk music of the southern United States. The boards were originally scraped with spoons and knives; their rasping rhythms became part of the musical stews known as Cajun and zydeco.

The washboard's use for laundry—and music—was in decline until musicians such as Clifton Chenier repopularized it in a new form. The wooden frame was discarded for a shoulder-strapped, chest-fitting piece of corrugated stainless steel. This lighter, streamlined scrub board became known as a **Frattoir** (*FRAH twah*). Its name probably comes from the French word *frotter,* which means "to rub."

Some *frattoir* players may still use knives or spoons, but often the scrapers of choice are cypress-handled bottle openers. These scratchers may see double duty when the music and gumbo are hot and the drinks are cold.

BEYOND

TRADITION

Why build an instrument when you can buy one?

This question was posed to me by an elementary school student and it stuck in my mind because it reflects on our specialized and industrialized society. We leave so much to the "experts." Sometimes this is good. But when we withdraw from participation in the everyday creativity of our lives, whether baking bread or playing music, something fundamental is lost.

Many world societies take it for granted that every human being is creative, and the idea of leaving music, dance, poetry—or any of the arts—to a chosen few, would be absurd. The creation of musical instruments can be as mysterious as music itself. Stories abound of how a given instrument was revealed to its inventor in a dream, or by God. While some instruments are clearly the pure invention of a single individual, many more are the culmination of ideas by countless contributors.

Musical inventors often combine the talents of musician and artisan in the forging of new instruments. Whatever their chosen medium—clay, steel, wood, animal skin, synthetics, or electronics—today's musical inventors share curiosity and a desire to create beautiful and unique musical objects. Some have perceived fresh possibilities in traditional instruments. Others have seen or heard something new in materials not previously used or never before combined. Through the process of discovery, invention, and reinvention, these artists and artisans transform musical instruments, building upon and beyond tradition.

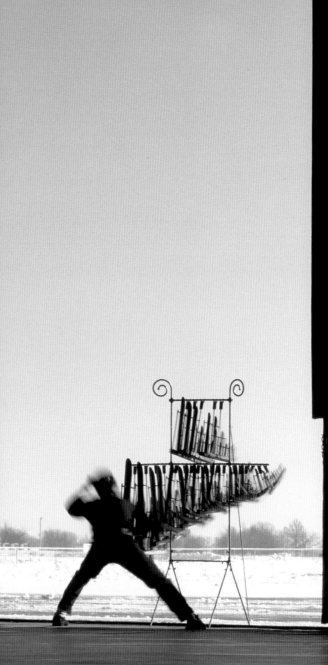

METAL ANGKLUNG

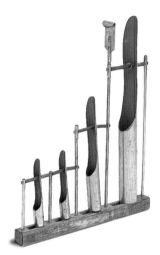

Each chime in a metal *angklung* is independently suspended within the frame. The chimes can be shaken or struck with the hands, causing the tones to swing in and out of rhythm with each other.

I n 1978, percussionist Robert Chappell was playing in a band that worked out of a union hall in an old mill town in rural Connecticut. One day, Chappell made his way to the hall's attic where he discovered an amazing instrument, cobwebbed and covered with the dust of years—a **Metal Angklung** (*AHNG klung*). At the time, he wasn't sure what it was. He asked some of the union hall members about the instrument's history and found that the original owner had played it in a vaudeville act. After the performer died in 1936, the *angklung* sat unplayed in the attic for forty-two years. The union members appreciated Chappell's enthusiasm and gave it to him as a gift.

Chappell researched the metal *angklung* and found that the J.C. Deagan Company of Chicago had once manufactured this and other metal instruments. They called it the "Deagan Organ Chimes." The following is a description from their catalog of the 1920s:

> A single tone or chime of "Deagan Organ Chimes" consists of four bell metal tubes mounted in a frame. The number of frames or chimes as specified mounted on a floor rack constitute a set, and the instrument is played by striking or shaking the same as sleigh bells.... "Deagan Organ Chimes" have a marvelously rich quadruple tone, very similar to that of a grand pipe organ.... "Deagan Organ Chimes" are universally conceded as being the greatest novelty instrument ever invented and can be played by from one to six performers according to the size and range.

Metal *angklungs* have not been produced for many years and are extremely rare—Chappell knows of only seven in existence. However, you may have seen one on television. The makers of *Star Trek: The Next Generation* were inspired to feature this antique yet futuristic instrument in one of their episodes, perhaps because of its strange, other-worldly beauty.

The design of the metal *angklung* was based on bamboo *angklung* instruments found in Indonesia.

OCEAN DRUM

Like the rainstick, the **Ocean Drum** strives to emulate the varied and elusive sounds of water. It is a frame drum with a synthetic, skin-like top head and a clear plastic bottom head. Sealed inside are steel pellets that roll across the surface of the head when the drum is tilted slightly. The resonant sound is like that of ocean waves. It has a calming, meditative effect and is fascinating to watch as the metal shot rolls across the head in fluid wave-like motions.

The ocean drum has many different voices to be explored—a snare-like sound, frame drum and tom tom effects, and a *cabasa*- or shaker-like tone. These can all be combined when playing the instrument in the traditional frame-drum manner, or when holding it between the player's legs bongo-style.

The ocean drum represents a love of natural sound and our attempts to capture the uncapturable—as if we could hold the sea in our hands.

"What was the first sound heard? It was the caress of the waters . . .

The mind must be slowed to catch the million transformations of the water, on sand, on shale, against driftwood, against the seawall. Each drop tinkles at a different pitch; each wave sets a different filtering on an inexhaustible supply of white noise."

—R. Murray Schafer, *The Soundscape*

THE WISE MAN DELIGHTS IN WATER.

—Lao-Tzu, *Tao Te Ching*

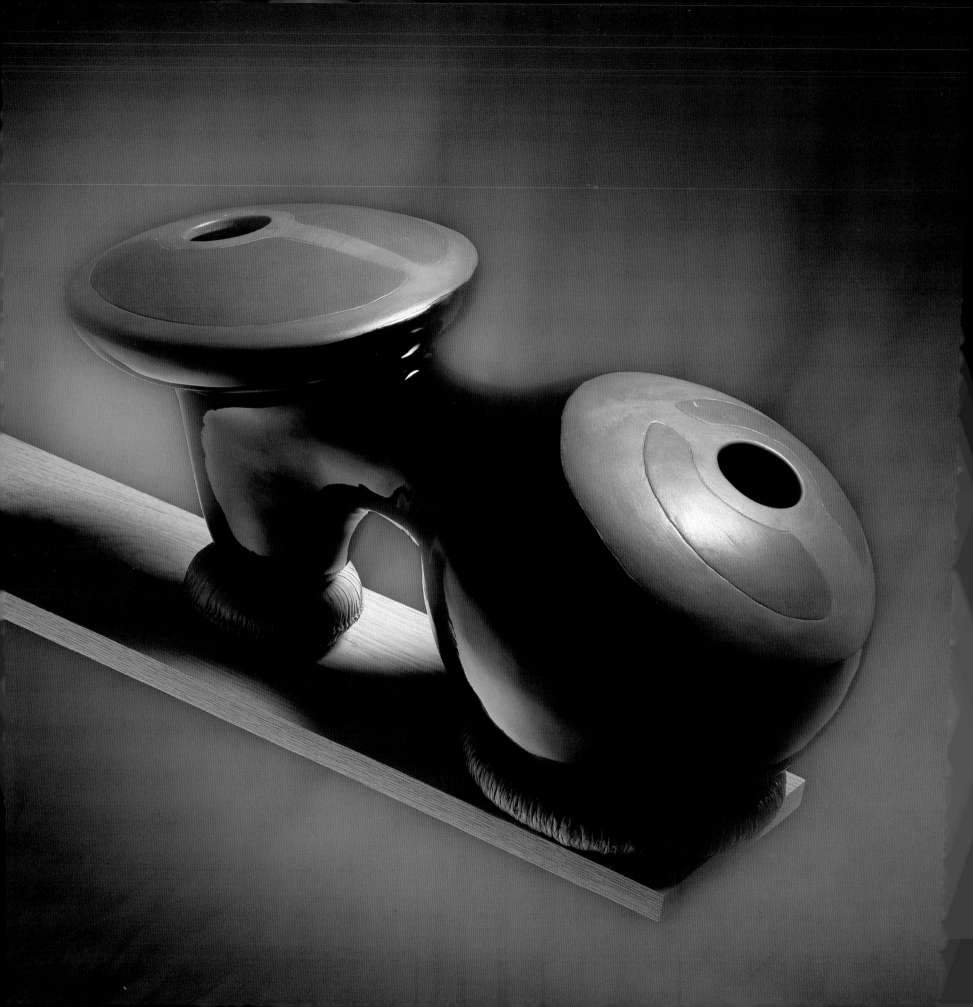

UDU DRUM

A drum that has no head? Headless drums do exist, in two countries thousands of miles apart. In India, such a drum is called *ghatam*. In Nigeria, it is called an **Udu Drum** (*oo doo*). *Udu* is the word for "pot" in the Ibo language of Nigeria. This clay pot drum is often made in the shape of a jug with a rounded bottom. Sometimes the ashes of family members are mixed into the clay of the drum. Thus the drum is sure to contain the voices of ancestral spirits.

Traditionally, *udu* drummers sit cradling the instrument in their lap. Sometimes it is played on woven rings set in front of the player. There are many different strokes—finger rolls, hand slaps, rubbing, and sliding—but the most novel and haunting sound is produced by opening and closing the side hole with the palm of the hand. This produces a warm bass tone reminiscent of dropping a stone into water.

Utilizing techniques learned from Abbas Ahuwan, a Nigerian master drum maker, Frank Giorgini combined his skills as folklorist, musician, and potter to create the inventive *udu* drum variations pictured here.

METAL
PERCUSSION

With torch and hammer, the muse is drawn from the metal. A metamorphosis occurs as a new instrument—foreign yet familiar—emerges from a shower of sparks.

In Brazil, it is not uncommon for percussionists to build their own metal instruments. Sometimes it is a matter of necessity, but often it is because the musicians prefer working with objects made to fit their own hands. Because of this, no two instruments will be identical and the state of the art is constantly changing.

It is in this spirit that **Metal Percussion** makers like Pete Engelhart work. His instruments have a wonderful tactile quality. They have a fine weight, and feel at home in your hand. The bird-like construction pictured here combines a *reco-reco* (Brazilian spring scraper) with two cowbells and a cymbal. It seems perpetually poised to hop from its perch and scamper off, clanging and clattering all the way. Through its unusual form and usefulness, it is an instrument that bridges the worlds of music and sculpture.

WATERPHONE

I f you are a fan of horror movies, you have heard the unsettling sounds of a **Waterphone**. This sculptural instrument was invented by Richard Waters. It consists of two bowls that have been welded together, creating a chamber into which a small amount of water is poured. Bronze rods of varying lengths are welded to the chamber's outer rim. These rods can be struck with different kinds of mallets, or drawn across with a double bass bow.

Holding the neck attached to the center of the chamber, one can shake and tilt the instrument while striking or bowing. This makes the water move inside the chamber. When the instrument is struck, the water "boings." When bowed, fluid and eerie glissandos come forth. It is just the sound for peering around dark corners, opening alien spacecrafts, or exploring the mysteries of the deep. The waterphone has also been used to communicate with whales and other cetaceans. When played in the ocean, its siren-like call has attracted pods of Orca whales who clearly respond to its kindred song.

NAIL MARIMBA

People around the world, by accident or intention, create musical instruments from everyday objects. Music can be coaxed from hub caps, bottle caps, yak horns, car horns, spoons, bones, conch shells, and bicycle bells. An antique Coca Cola sign may find a second life as a gong. A circle of metal mixing bowls can become a cookware *gamelan*. Unique instruments such as these inspire us to make our own music, and to discover the music hidden in ordinary things.

Michael Meadows, a craftsman by trade, is an instrument maker and player by inclination. He has constructed wands that whistle, plumbing that sings, and a xylophone of glass. His **Nail Marimba** consists of a resonating box with a sound hole on the bottom. Nails are hammered into the box at varying lengths to create different pitches. The nails, when struck with thin sticks, have a suprising melodic richness, like that of a wooden marimba.

WOODEN DRUMS

The art of making **Wooden Drums** has undergone a renaissance in the United States. Many instrument makers, professional and amateur alike, have rediscovered the pleasure and expressive potential in constructing drums from wood and skin. Thus we find *bodhrans* made in Pennsylvania, American Indian drums from New Mexico, West African–influenced *ashikos* built in Vermont, and *djembes* carved in California.

In Montana, drum maker Paula Allegrini has drawn inspiration from African and American Indian sources to create the drums pictured here. They are fashioned from domestic hardwoods and skins of deer, elk, moose, or cow.

Allegrini and fellow drum makers are revisiting the age-old practice of drum building—forming the shells, curing and stretching the skins, infusing the instruments with personality and spirit, and making them their own.

SOUND SCULPTURES

Sound Sculptures are multisensory objects, as fascinating to see or touch as they are to hear. Many of us experience them every day in the form of wind chimes. These are musical mobiles, instruments of air and chance. Artists from different disciplines, such as Swiss sculptor Jean Tinguely and American architect Harry Bertoia, have created massive musical sculptures as permanent installations in public places—shopping malls, courtyards, and parks.

Ward Hartenstein works on a smaller scale. He is a sculptor of clay. In his hands, it is molded into bells, bowls, and bars. He has developed a wide variety of sound sculptures—from suspended, intricate clay chimes, to more streamlined tubes and bells. His "fountain chime" (pictured here) is played by dropping steel pellets into a clear acrylic tube. The pellets cascade over and around a column of clay chimes, finally gathering in a large dish at its base. The rhythms are unpredictable—dependent on the number and velocity of the pellets dropped, coupled with the elements of gravity and caprice. The resulting sound evokes a child's marble maze or some sort of futuristic rainstick.

WAVEDRUM

Sound is vibration. Vibrations are waves: short or long, wide or narrow. A pure sound wave is constant, perfect, and decidedly uninteresting. What gives sound its personality is how the wave is formed and what is added to it, just as spice is added to a meal.

Pictured here is an electronic percussion instrument called a **Wavedrum**. Its sounds are generated by mathematically created models of the wave forms of various percussion instruments and sound effects. Take, for example, the *udu* drum program of the wavedrum. Just as with a true ceramic drum, the wavedrum reacts responsively to the player's variations of touch and intensity, and where the drum is struck influences tone and pitch. This may be the first electric drum designed to be played with the fingers, though sticks and mallets can also be used to great effect. Its sound palette ranges from tabla to thunderstorm.

It would seem that the wavedrum is a long way from bullroarers and hollowed logs. And yet music and rhythm are in a constant state of change and evolution. This is but another branch of the drummer's path, another means of expressing the same impulse—to invent, to create, to drum!

RHYTHM
NEVER ENDS

Looking back through this book, I am reminded of the story of the blind men and the elephant. Each man thought he could understand the whole animal by touching only a single part. "An elephant is like a wall," said one, touching the side of the beast. "No, no. An elephant is like a fan," exclaimed another, feeling one of the great ears. "You're both wrong," interjected the third, holding the sinewy trunk in his hands. "Anyone can tell you that an elephant is exactly like a snake."

So it is with this book of percussion. It covers a subject so vast that it can only be glimpsed in small parts—with each of those parts a world inside a world, a microcosm of rhythm.

My perception of these instruments is always changing. Sometimes they are beautiful objects, abstracted from their musical use. Then I will see them in their cultural and geographical contexts: as common as a teapot, or as foreign as a new language. Then again, my focus will change and they become far-flung members of the same family, distant cousins charged with rhythmic possibility. Perhaps more than sound, what they share is silence—the electric silence that precedes the first downbeat.

Finally, it all comes back to the simple pleasure of percussion—shaking, twirling, plucking, or hitting something, and liking the sound—the noise becoming rhythm and the rhythm becoming music.

Somewhere a percussionist is always playing. A *bendir* buzzes by a desert fire. *Mbiras* echo from a roundhouse in Zimbabwe. The *bodhran* player strikes up a jig in a smoky Dublin pub. A tympanist meticulously tunes before a concert in Warsaw. A Brazilian street is flooded with hundreds of samba players. The notes of a *gamelan* hang like clouds in the lush air of a Javanese night. And a young drummer sweats over a snare drum in an American garage. The sun sets on one land and rises on another, but rhythm never ends.

SUGGESTED READING

ESPECIALLY FOR CHILDREN

··

Suggested readings on simple instrument making and playing:

—De Beer, Sara, ed. **Open Ears**. Roslyn, NY: Ellipsis Kids, 1995.

—Drew, Helen. **My First Music Book**. London: Dorling Kindersley, 1993.

—Dworsky, Alan. **Conga Drumming: A Beginner's Guide to Playing with Time**. Book/CD. Minnetonka, MN: Dancing Hands Music, 1994.

—Hopkins, Bart. **Making Simple Musical Instruments**. Asheville, NC: Lark Books, 1995.

—James, Ben. **Have Fun Playing Hand Drums**. Book/CD. Brattleboro, VT: InterWorld Music, 1998.

Almeida, Bira. **Capoeira: A Brazilian Art Form: History, Philosophy and Practice**. Berkeley, CA: North Atlantic Books, 1986. A fascinating and personal study.

Bebey, Francis. **African Music: A People's Art**. Trans. by Josephine Bennett. New York: Lawrence Hill & Co., 1997. A study of African music from an African point of view.

Beck, John H., ed. **Encyclopedia of Percussion**. New York: Garland Publishing, 1997. A useful reference source of percussion instruments and terms.

Blades, James. **Percussion Instruments and Their History**. Westport, CT: Bold Strummer, 1997. First published in 1970, this book may be on more percussionists' bookshelves than any other. An overview of Western and non-Western percussion.

Broughton, Simon, ed. **World Music: The Rough Guide**. London: Rough Guides, Ltd., 1994. A breezy and surprisingly comprehensive introduction to popular and traditional music from the Andes to Zimbabwe. Includes articles on artists, instruments, and recordings.

Diallo, Yaya with Mitchell Hall. **The Healing Drum: African Wisdom Teachings**. Rochester, VT: Destiny Books, 1989. An interesting study of West African rhythm and culture.

Hart, Mickey with Jay Stevens. **Drumming at the Edge of Magic: A Journey into the Spirit of Percussion**. San Francisco: Acid Test, 1998. The Grateful Dead percussionist's compelling autobiographical journey into the heart of percussion.

Jaffe, Nina. **Patakin: World Tales of Drums and Drummers**. New York: Henry Holt & Co., 1994. A storyteller's collection of drum tales and myths. Informative and entertaining for all ages.

Mathieu, W. A. **The Musical Life: Reflections on What It Is and How to Live It**. Boston and London: Shambhala, 1994. Essays on musical perception and its applications in everyday life.

Nettl, Bruno, et al. **Excursions in World Music**. Englewood Cliffs, NJ: Prentice Hall, 1996. A good introduction to many major musical traditions of the world. Available with a compact disc.

Reck, David. **Music of the Whole Earth**. New York: Da Capo Press, 1997. An accessible and rewarding book, covering a vast range of musical traditions and addressing the mechanics of music and musical instruments.

Redmond, Layne. **When the Drummers Were Women: A Spiritual History of Rhythm.** New York: Crown Publishing, 1997. Frame drummer Layne Redmond combines history, mythology, musical lore, and personal experience to explore and reassert the importance of women in the history of drumming.

Schafer, R. Murray. **The Soundscape: Our Sonic Environment and the Tuning of the World.** Rochester, VT: Destiny Books, 1994. A pioneering work, originally published in 1976, concerning the connection of sound and environment.

Wilson, Sule Greg. **The Drummer's Path: Moving the Spirit with Ritual and Traditional Drumming.** Rochester, VT: Destiny Books, 1992. A passionate study of African and African diaspora drumming. Available with compact disc.

PERIODICALS

Experimental Musical Instruments—A quarterly publication dedicated to new and experimental instruments. Experimental Musical Instruments, P.O. Box 784, Nicasio, CA 94946. (415) 662-2182.

Modern Drummer Magazine—A magazine primarily aimed at drummers and drum set players. Occasionally features articles on other types of percussion as well as a monthly listing of new products. Modern Drummer, Subscriptions, P.O. Box 480, Mt. Morris, IL 61054. (800) 551-3786.

Percussive Notes and **Percussion News**—Both published bimonthly by the Percussive Arts Society, a not-for-profit organization for drummers and percussionists. Percussive Arts Society, P.O. Box 25, Lawton, OK 73502. (580) 353-1455.

Rhythm Magazine—An excellent monthly magazine covering many styles of music from around the world. *Percussion Source*, published twice a year, is an additional resource that includes a guide to world percussion teachers in the United States. Rhythm Magazine, 928 Broadway, Suite 204, New York, NY 10010. (800) 464-2767.

RECOMMENDED VIDEOS

·······························

From InterWorld Music, www.interworld.com (800) 698-6705:

Robin Anders, **Voices of the Doumbek**

John Bergamo, **The Art and Joy of Hand Drumming**

Mel Mercier with Seamus Egan, **Bodhran and Bones**

Tony Vacca, **Melodic Percussion**

Glen Velez, **Fantastic World of Frame Drums**

And from Talking Drums, www.talkingdrum.com (800) 253-3786:

Paulo Mattioli, **African Percussion**

Airto Moreira, **Brazilian Percussion**

SUGGESTED LISTENING

MULTI-PERCUSSION

The Big Bang (Ellipsis Arts...). A great place to start your journey into world percussion listening. The three-CD set with booklet includes over three hours of global percussion. Well selected and documented.

Ibuki by Kodo (Tristar). A fine introduction to the music of one of Japan's premiere percussion ensembles.

Serpentine by Keith Terry & Crosspulse (Ubiquity). A cross-cultural collection of world and body percussion works.

Mapa by Uakti (Point Music). This Brazilian ensemble performs with invented and handmade instruments.

Planet Drum (Rykodisc). Mickey Hart's Grammy award–winning collection showcasing world percussionists. Hart's companion book by the same title is also recommended.

Opus 1 by the Pan African Orchestra (Real World). Ghanaian bell and drum playing.

BALAFON

Djelika by Toumani Diabate (Hannibal). Malian *balafon* virtuoso Keletigui Diabate accompanies the string instruments *kora* and *ngomi* in a beautiful, unadorned recording.

Harare to Kisingani by Balafon Marimba Ensemble (Shanachie). Mallet music from Zimbabwe.

BERIMBAU

Capoeira Angola from Salvador, Brazil by Grupo De Capoeira Angola Pelourinho (Smithsonian Folkways). Traditional ensemble *capoeira* music.

Capoeira by Guilherme Franco (Lyrichord). A mix of solo and group pieces featuring the *berimbau* and the double *berimbau,* which Franco invented.

BODHRAN

Chieftains 4 by the Chieftains (Shanachie). This and other recordings by the traditional Irish group feature *bodhran* playing.

CONGA & BONGOS

....

Ritmo Y Candela (Tonga). Carlos "Patato" Valdes, Jose Luis "Changuito" Quintana, Orestes Vilato, and others are featured in this Latin percussion session.

Conga Blue by Pancho Sanchez (Concord Picante). *Conquero* Pancho Sanchez pays tribute to the great Mongo Santamaria.

FRAME DRUM

....

Assyrian Rose by Glen Velez (CMP).

Trio Globo (Silver Wave Records).

Both of these frame drum recordings display masterful work by Glen Velez, a founding member of Trio Globo. On "Assyrian Rose" he is joined by Layne Redmond.

GAMELAN

....

Bali: Gamelan and Kecak (Elektra/Nonesuch).

Javanese Court Gamelan (Elektra/Nonesuch).

Jegog: The Rhythmic Power of Bamboo by Nyoman Jayus Bamboo Ensemble (Multicultural Media).

Music for the Gods: The Fahnestock South Seas Expedition (Rykodisc). Mostly Balinese gamelan music in state-of-the-art performances recorded in the 1940s.

MBIRA

....

Shona Spirit by Dumisani Maraire and Ephat Mujura (Music of the World). Duets by *mbira* masters.

The Soul of Mbira: Music and Traditions of the Shona People of Zimbabwe (Nonesuch Records). The companion CD to Paul Berliner's excellent book of the same name.

STEEL PAN

....

The Long Time Band by Andy Narell (Windham Hill). Contemporary steel pan music.

Pan Woman (Delos). Various steel bands from Trinidad and Tobago.

TABLA & GHATAM

....

The Best of Shakti by Shakti (Moment Records). East meets West in this fusion of jazz and Indian classical music. Features acoustic guitar, violin, tabla, and *ghatam*.

Tabla Tarang: Melody on Drums by Pandit Kamalesh Maitra with Trilobe Gurtu (Smithsonian Folkways).

TALKING DRUM

....

In Search of the Lost Riddim by Ernest Ranglin (Palm Pictures). Jamaican jazz guitarist Ernest Ranglin plays with Senegalese percussion greats.

Juju Music by King Sunny Ade (Mango). Talking drum–driven Nigerian pop.

AUDIO CD SONG LIST

The music on the enclosed audio compact disc has been selected and recorded expressly for this book. While a few of the selections are traditional, most are original compositions by the artists and are meant to showcase a selection of the instruments found in these pages.

1 Gathering Song (Rocky Maffit, Neal Robinson) 4:38
This piece begins with a chant that is reminiscent of harvest songs from various cultures. In this case it is a gathering not of crops, but of percussion. The buzzing sound you hear in the background is the signature sound of the *bendir*.

Amasong (Champaign-Urbana's Premier Lesbian/Feminist Chorus), conducted by Kristina Boerger: vocals. Rocky Maffit: ankle rattles, *bendir*, vocals. Patience Mudeka: vocals. Neal Robinson: ankle rattles, keyboards.

Solos—Robert Chappell: tabla. Bill Herriot: saxophone. Rocky Maffit: cowbell, *doumbek*, maraca, *sistrum*, talking drum, vocal percussion, wavedrum. Neal Robinson: keyboards (*karimba* samples), vocal percussion. Patricia Sandler: *berimbau*.

2 Metal Angels (Robert Chappell) 2:02
This is a rare solo recording of a metal *angklung*. Robert Chappell sets the chimes swinging by striking and shaking them.

Robert Chappell: metal *angklung*.

3 Udu Time (Rocky Maffit) 2:06
I entered the studio with boxes of beautiful new *udu* drums—and improvised. The *ocarina* melodies were inspired by central African Pygmy vocalizations.

Rocky Maffit: clay *ocarina*, *udu* drums (*mbwata*, *udongo*, *kim kim*, and *utar*). Neal Robinson: clay *ocarina*.

4 Amai (Tendai Handina) 2:35
Zimbabwean musician and dancer Patience Mudeka contributed this lovely song. Its joyous sound disguises lyrics of longing and homesickness. *Amai* means "mother" in the Shona language.

Rocky Maffit: cowbell, shakers, *surdu* (left speaker), talking drum (right speaker). Patience Mudeka: vocals. Neal Robinson: keyboards.

5 Bamboo Mountain (Rocky Maffit) 2:22
The swelling roar of a Chinese wind gong is followed by the call and response
of handheld bamboo *angklung* rattles.

> Rocky Maffit: bamboo *angklung*, bamboo pan flute, *bin-sasara*, gong, rainsticks, rattles.

6 Amadinda (Tigger Benford, Bill Herriot) 2:16
This selection combines traditional Ugandan *amadinda* playing with a jazz-like
tenor saxophone improvisation.

> Tigger Benford: *amadinda*. Rex Benincasa: *amadinda*. Bill Herriot: saxophone. Martha
> Partridge: *amadinda*. Recording of *amadinda* engineered by Peter Karl.

7 Hello Goodbye (John Lennon, Paul McCartney) 3:26
Brazilian *berimbau* meets the Beatles. Body percussion and tambourine provide
the rhythmic accompaniment.

> Kristina Boerger: vocals. Rocky Maffit: *berimbau*, body percussion, tambourine, vocals.
> Patricia Sandler: *berimbau*. © 1967 Sony/ATV Songs LLC, BMI. Used by permission.

8 Holding the Sea (Rocky Maffit) 3:18
This is an exploration of the rhythmic and tonal possibilities of the ocean drum.

> Rocky Maffit: ocean drum.

9 Memory Park (Rocky Maffit) 2:14
A musical evocation of conga and bongo players in the park. The *djembe* is featured
as a solo instrument.

> Rocky Maffit: bongos, congas, *djembe*, metal percussion, *shekere*, vocals.

10 Yoobi (Oscar Sulley Braimah, Neal Robinson) 5:05
Yoobi, a Ghanaian expression meaning "good heart," is a fusion of West African
bells and American slide guitar.

> Oscar Sulley Braimah: *gankogui*, vocals. Keith Harden: *dobro*. Rocky Maffit: bells (African
> and Latin), cymbals, *shekere*, vocals. Neal Robinson: bells (African and Latin), keyboards.

11 **Two Times** (Ed Harrison) 2:31
The title refers to the two time signatures contained in this improvisation by maraca virtuoso Ed Harrison.

Ed Harrison: maracas.

12 **Bangeza** (traditional) 3:31
In this song, the *mbira* is played inside a calabash resonator. The gourd, ornamented with bottlecaps, creates a buzzing that Tom Turino likens to the sound of a torn stereo speaker.

Tom Turino: *mbira* (with calabash), vocals.

13 **Cracked Earth** (Patricia Sandler) 4:55
In Zimbabwe, *mbiras* are often played in pairs, with each player executing different interlocking parts. This song takes an unconventional approach—both parts are performed by South African *mbirist* Patricia Sandler.

Rocky Maffit: ankle rattles, seedpods. Neal Robinson: keyboards. Patricia Sandler: *mbiras*.

14 **Gathering Song** (reprise) 1:41
A return to our opening theme, harmonically restated on the keyboards with the *bendirs* and tabla thundering back in.

Robert Chappell: tabla. Rocky Maffit: *bendir,* vocals. Neal Robinson: keyboards.

15 **Elegiac** (Peter Jones, Tigger Benford) 5:14
The classical percussion of East and West, tabla and piano, converse in this haunting jazz- and gospel-influenced lament.

Tigger Benford: tabla. Peter Jones: piano. Recorded by Joe Podlesny.

Produced by Rocky Maffit and Neal Robinson. Recorded and mixed by Neal Robinson at DayGroup and Highcross AV studios in Urbana, Illinois, unless otherwise noted. Mastering and editing for the compact disc was provided by Jonathan D. Pines at Private Studios. A technical note: Tracks 2, 8, 11, 12, and 15 were all recorded live, with no overdubbing. All compositions © 1999 by composers unless otherwise noted. Maffit compositions © 1999 Maffit Music, BMI.

The producers give their thanks to all the musicians and composers who contributed so graciously to this project.

PERCUSSION SOURCES

One does not have to travel abroad to find examples of the percussion instruments featured in this book; there are many fine instrument makers and music shops right here in the United States. Below is a contact list, including artists and artisans whose work appears in this book.

Afena Akoma African Instruments
250 Cumberland Street, Suite 203, Rochester, NY 14605. (800) 982-3362 or (716) 325-3790. www.afenaakoma.com. *Mail order and store.*

African Percussion
115 S. Topanga Canyon Boulevard, #169, Topanga, CA 90290. (800) 733-3786. www.pacificnet.net/~drum1/. *Mail order.*

African Rhythm Traders
825 NE Broadway, Portland, OR 97232. (800) 894-9149 or (503) 288-6950. www.rhythmtraders.com. *Store.*

Paul Aljian Drumworks
98 Grayson Place, Teaneck, NJ 07666. (201) 833-4550. *Frame drum and doumbek maker.*

All One Tribe Drums
P.O. Box "Drawer N," Taos, NM 87571. (800) 442-3786. www.allonetribedrum.com. *Mail order.*

Paula Allegrini
c/o Moondance, P.O. Box 8592, Missoula, MT 59807. (406) 777-1344. *Wooden drum maker.*

Anyone Can Whistle
323 Wall Street, Kingston, NY 12401. (914) 331-7728. *Store.*

Atlanta Drums and Percussion
1776 NE Expressway, Atlanta, GA 30329. (404) 633-4070. *Store.*

Bon Cajun Instruments
886 McMillan, Iota, LA 70543. (318) 779-2456. *Frattoir and Cajun percussion maker.*

Bookalaka Imports
4786 Excelente Drive, Woodland Hills, CA 91364. (800) 873-0992. *Mail order.*

Dennis Capodestria
Box 424, Ashland, NH 03217. (603) 968-3145. *Mbira maker.*

Centre Street Drums
342 Centre Street, Brockton, MA 02402. (508) 559-5112. *Store.*

Coyote Paw Gallery
6388 Delmar Boulevard, St. Louis, MO 63130. (314) 721-7576. *Store.*

Drum Brothers
P.O. Box 678, Arlee, MT 59821. (800) 925-1201. *African-style hand drum maker.*

(Continued from previous page)

Drummers World
151 West 46th Street, New York,
NY 10036. (212) 840-3057. *Store.*

Drums on the Web.com
23 Waverly Place, Suite 65,
New York, NY 10003. (212) 254-1133.
www.drumsontheweb.com. *Internet store.*

Earthshaking Music
P. O. Box 18372, 1287 Glenwood Avenue,
Suite D, Atlanta, GA 30316. (888) 978-2500
or (404) 622-0707. *Mail order and store.*

Pete Engelhart
1507 Second Street, Berkeley, CA 94710.
(510) 845-5061. *Metal percussion maker.*

Everyone's Drumming
P.O. Box 361, Putney, VT 05346.
(800) 326-0726 or (802) 387-2249.
www.everyonesdrumming.com.
African-style hand drum maker.

Final Chants Music Co.
415 "I" Street, Arcata, CA 95521.
(800) 554-3786. *Mail order.*

Frank Georgini
c/o UDU Drums, Route 67, Box 126,
Freehold, NY 12431. (800) 838-3786 or
(518) 634-2559. *Udu drum maker.*

The Gourd Connection
3210 Garrison Street, San Diego, CA 92106.
(619) 224-1378. www.menehune.com/
thegourdconnection/. *Hawaiian gourd
drum maker.*

Ward Hartenstein
244 Edgerton Street, Rochester,
NY 14607. (716) 271-8529.
Sound sculpture maker.

The House of Musical Traditions
7040 Carroll Avenue, Takoma Park, MD
20912. (800) 540-379 or (301) 270-9090.
www.hmtrad.com. *Mail order and store.*

John's Music
4501 Interlake Avenue North, #9,
Seattle, WA 98103. (800) 473-5194 or
(206) 548-0916. *Store.*

Korg USA, Inc.
316 S. Service Road, Melville, NY 11747.
(516) 333-9100. www.korg.com.
Wavedrum maker.

Lark in the Morning
P.O. Box 1176, Mendocino, CA 95460.
(707) 964-5569. *Mail order and stores
in Mendocino, CA, and Seattle, WA.*

Latin Percussion (LP) Music Group
World Beat Percussion Division,
160 Belmont Avenue, Garfield, NJ 07026.
(800) 526-0508 or (973) 478-6903.
Latin percussion maker.

Michael Meadows
22918 Stevens Street, Madison, WI 53705.
(608) 233-2937. *Nail marimba maker.*

Mid-East Manufacturing, Inc.
7694 Progress Circle, West Melbourne,
FL 32904. (407) 724-1477. www.mid-
east.com. *Indian-style percussion maker.*

Noisy Toys
8728 ¼ S. Sepulveda Boulevard,
Westchester, CA 90083. (800) 874-8223.
www.noisytoys.com. *Store.*

Other Ports
120 North Street, Normal, IL 61761.
(309) 454-5071. *Store.*

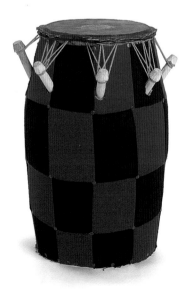

Panyard, Inc.
1216 California Avenue, Akron,
OH 44314. (800) 377-0202 or (330) 745-
3155. www.panyard.com. *Steel pan maker.*

Passport To Peru
1806 Coventry Road, Cleveland Heights,
OH 44118. (216) 932-9783. *Store.*

Percussion East
P.O. Box 1629, Southampton, PA 18966.
(215) 555-1212. www.threebirds.com.
Mail order and store.

Planetary Percussion
1322 Grand Avenue, Glenwood Springs, CO
81601. (888) 385-8726. *Mail order and store.*

ProDrum & Percussion Center
363 N. Easton Road, Glenside, PA 19038.
(215) 887-1462. *Mail order and store.*

REMO, Inc.
28101 Industry Drive, Valencia, CA 91355.
(800) 525-5134 or (805) 294-5600.
www.remo.com. *Ocean drum maker.*

Rhythm Fusion
1541-C Pacific Avenue, Santa Cruz,
CA 95060. (408) 423-2048. *Mail order
and store.*

Rolling Thunder
2631 Barcells Avenue, Santa Clara, CA
95051. (408) 247-5662. www.taiko.com.
Mail order taiko drums.

Skins and Tins
29 Main Street, Champaign, IL 61820.
(217) 352-3786. *Store.*

Steve Weiss Music
2324 Wyandotte Road, Willow Grove,
PA 19090. (215) 324-3999. *Mail order.*

Talking Drums
863B South Elm Street, Greensboro,
NC 27406. (800) 253-3786.
www.talkingdrums.com. *Mail order and store.*

Taos Drums
P.O. Box 1916, Taos, NM 87571.
(800) 424-3786. *American Indian
percussion maker.*

Maximo B. Teppa
c/o Ed Harrison, 946 Wenonah Avenue,
Oak Park, IL 60304. (708) 848-8904.
Maraca maker.

Richard Waters
P.O. Box 1071, Pahoa, HI 96778.
(808) 622-1431. *Waterphone maker.*

West Cliff Percussion
2575 Mission Street, Santa Cruz, CA
95060. (831) 454-0345. *African-style
hand drum maker.*

West Music
P.O. Box 5521, 1212 Fifth Street,
Coralville, IA 52241. (800) 397-9378 or
(319) 351-2000. www.westmusic.com.
Mail order and four stores.

Peter Whitehead
c/o Strange Attractor Studio, 455A Valencia
Street, San Francisco, CA 94103.
(415) 621-8906. *Instrument maker.*

The Wright Hand Drum Co.
15 Sycamore Street, Hagerstown,
MD 21740. (800) 990-4263.
www.wrighthanddrums.com.
Ceramic drum maker.

Zephyr Drum Co.
P.O. Box 22693, Santa Fe,
NM 87502. (800) 488-3402 or
(505) 982-3402. www.adam-inc.org.
Ceramic drum maker.

ACKNOWLEDGMENTS

Grateful acknowledgment is made to the following for permission to reprint from previously published works:

Balafon legend (page 25) from *The Healing Drum* by Yaya Diallo with Mitchell Hall. © 1989 Yaya Diallo and Mitchell Hall. Reprinted by permission of Inner Traditions International, Ltd.

Berimbau historical background (page 27) from *Drumming at the Edge of Magic* by Mickey Hart with Jay Stevens. © 1998 Mickey Hart. Reprinted by permission of Acid Test Productions.

Quotation (page 45) from *The Mambo Kings Play Songs of Love* by Oscar Hijuelos. © 1989 Oscar Hijuelos. Reprinted by permission of Farrar, Straus & Giroux, Inc. and Harriet Wasserman Literary Agency, Inc.

Slit drum descriptions (page 48) from *African Music: A People's Art* by Francis Bebey. English language edition translated by Josephine Bennett © 1997 Lawrence Hill & Co., Publishers, Inc. Originally published as *Musique de L'Afrique* © 1969 Horizons de France. Reprinted by permission of Lawrence Hill Books, an imprint of Chicago Review Press, Inc.

Tabla story (page 55) and *bodhran* legend (page 75) from *Patakin: World Tales of Drums and Drummers* by Nina Jaffe. © 1994 Nina Jaffe. Reprinted by permission of Henry Holt and Company, Inc.

"Tambourines" (page 72) by Langston Hughes. © 1994 by the Estate of Langston Hughes. Reprinted by permission of Harold Ober Associates Incorporated.

Scripture (page 73) excerpted from the *Holy Bible, New International Version.* © 1973, 1978, 1984 by International Bible Society. Reprinted by permission of Zondervan Publishing House.

Sistrum historical background (page 89) from *Percussion Instruments and Their History* by James Blades. © 1997 The Bold Strummer Ltd. Reprinted by permission of The Bold Strummer Ltd.

Quotations (page 105) from *The Soundscape: Our Sonic Environment and the Tuning of the World* by R. Murray Schafer. © 1977, 1994 R. Murray Schafer. Originally appeared in *The Tuning of the World* published by Alfred A. Knopf, Inc. Reprinted by permission of Inner Traditions International, Ltd. and R. Murray Schafer.

This is a book filled with circles: drum circles, circles of sound, and circles of friends. In fact, one of my deepest pleasures while working on this project has been the rekindling of past friendships and the beginning of new ones. As I suspect it is with other passions, when one digs beneath the surface one discovers a patchwork community of fascinating and generous people—in this case, a fellowship of music.

My thanks to all who shared their time, talent, instruments, and expertise in the creation of this project: David Akins, Paula Allegrini, Midao Gideon Foli Alorwoyie, Tigger Benford, Rex Benincasa, Kristina Boerger and Amasong, Oscar Sulley Braimah, Arlene Brown, Dennis Capodestria, Robert Chappell, Danielle Ciardullo and Korg USA, Rena Day, Edward Durkin, Pete Engelhart, Fred Fairchild, Frank Giorgini, Ingrid Gordon, Keith Harden, Ed Harrison, Ward Hartenstein, Liz and Terry Hawkins, Bill Herriot, Stephen Hill, Bill and Lydia Hohulin, Patti and Michael Johnson, Peter Jones, Peter Karl, Jim Kishline, John Levin, Sean Little Rabbit, Little Wind, Michael Meadows, Chris Mhlanga, Chuck Mlecko, Chris Morosin, Patience Mudeka, Bruno Nettl, Martha Partridge, Jonathan D. Pines, Jarrad Powell, Morgan and Patricia Hruby Powell, Michael Powers, Naomi Rempe, Mark Rubel, Joyce Sameshima of Kokyo Taiko and the Buddhist Temple of Chicago, Patricia Sandler, Anna Schultz, Wayne Silas Sr., Thomas Siwe, Bob Steinman, Sumaryono, Clara Sweet, Liam Teague, Edward and Nancy Tepper, Tom Turino, Richard Waters, the music library of the University of Illinois, and everyone at the Champaign and Urbana public libraries.

Special thanks to Michael Day and Evelyn Glennie, and to the book production team, especially Randee Bowlin, Ellen Greene, Kim Grossmann, and Julie Mazur.

And finally my deepest appreciation to: Bob Nirkind, for taking on this project; Neal Robinson, for his enduring friendship and limitless musical talent; Kate Kuper, whose invisible hand lies behind every word; Chris Brown, for his singular artistry, his faith, and his friendship; project editor Becky Mead, for her questions and clarity; and Evelyn Shapiro, who took me seriously when I casually suggested that I had an idea for a book on percussion. Without her vision, and artistic and organizational skills, this book simply would not exist. I also wish to thank the Kuper and Maffit families whose love and faith have sustained me through the changing tides of a musical life.

INDEX